# gary heery

KÖNEMANN

Tiger, *tiger*, burning bright
forests of the night,
and or eye

d frame thy fearful symmetry?
William Blake

Why?   It's a question I asked myself more than once during the two years it's taken to put these photographs together. I asked it watching a lioness rip the hell out of six hundred dollars worth of canvas backdrop, having first, with critical economy, peed on it. I asked it as the white rhino stood bum to camera for a myopic eternity staring at a similarly expensive backdrop and then horned into it. As I drove to Dubbo for the fourth time to try to nail that same rhino, I asked the question again. And again when the male mute swan decided to kill me, and again when I stepped in wet tiger poo—perhaps the worst smell on earth. When my face and camera were covered in a monster spider web of giraffe saliva I almost stopped asking it. At least the giraffe was being friendly. After experiencing the Richter—scaling, electrifying eternity of the African elephant's fart, the question ceased to seem relevant.

Warum?   Diese Frage habe ich mir in den zwei Jahren, in denen diese Fotosammlung entstand, mehr als einmal gestellt. Ich stellte sie mir, während ich einer Löwin dabei zusah, wie sie eine sechshundert Dollar teure Dekoleinwand in kleine Fetzen zerriß, die sie zuvor mit kunstverständiger Sparsamkeit bepinkelt hatte. Ich stellte mir diese Frage, während das weiße Nashorn eine Ewigkeit mit dem Hinterteil zur Kamera stand, kurzsichtig auf einen ähnlich teuren Hintergrund starrte und schließlich doch sein Horn hineinbohrte. Als ich zum vierten Mal nach Dubbo fuhr, um dasselbe Nashorn endlich vor die Linse zu bekommen, habe ich mir die Frage wieder gestellt. Ich stellte sie mir, als der männliche Höckerschwan sich entschloß, mich zu töten, und noch einmal, als ich in einen frischen Tigerhaufen trat — der wahrscheinlich schlimmste Gestank auf Erden. Als mein Gesicht und meine Kamera von einem gigantischen Spinnennetz aus Giraffenspucke bedeckt waren, habe ich fast aufgehört zu fragen — immerhin hatte die Giraffe es nett gemeint. Und nachdem ich den Furz des Afrikanischen Elefanten miterlebt hatte — der jedes Leben erstarren läßt, eine kleine Ewigkeit dauert und mit Sicherheit auf der Richter-Skala meßbar ist —, verlor das Warum jegliche Bedeutung.

Pourquoi ?   Cette question, je me la suis posée plus d'une fois durant les deux années que j'ai consacrées à réaliser ces photographies. Je me la suis posée en contemplant une lionne lacérer, après l'avoir consciencieusement souillée d'urine, une toile de fond qui m'avait coûté six cents dollars. Je me la suis posée quand le rhinocéros blanc ne consentit qu'à présenter son arrière-train à l'appareil photo pour contempler pendant une éternité de myopie une toile de fond tout aussi onéreuse avant de l'éperonner d'un coup de corne. Lorsque je me rendis pour la quatrième fois à Dubbo afin d'essayer de fixer sur la pellicule ce même rhinocéros, je me la suis de nouveau posée. Et encore la fois où le cygne muet mâle décida de me tuer ou quand je marchai dans des excréments de tigre encore humides — l'odeur sans doute la plus épouvantable qui soit. Quand mon visage et mon appareil photographique ont été inondés par une gigantesque toile d'araignée de salive de girafe, j'ai failli cesser de me la poser. Au moins, la girafe était-elle amicale. Après avoir connu les effets dévastateurs, mesurables sur l'échelle de Richter, du pet de l'éléphant d'Afrique, la question cessa de me paraître pertinente.

I claim no special affinity for animals. Asthma means I can't even have a dog or cat and the relationship with my daughter's budgie isn't exactly a threat to Dr Doolittle. As a kid I was taken to Taronga Zoo perhaps twice a year. My mum has a Fifties photograph of me at the zoo holding a rabbit. I can't recall the animals—what I most remember about the day is the fistfight I had with my cousin Wilfred. I won.

I grew up in Sydney's Double Bay. In those days it wasn't the trough of the face-lifted, triple-parking, born-to-shop crowd. Mum did a little SP bookmaking at home and I'd sometimes have to run the bets. On summer nights when the nor'westerly was blowing, it was possible to lie in bed and hear a strange, haunting sound floating across the harbour. It was the roar of the zoo lions in their sad concrete pits. Perhaps because I knew the conditions in which they and many of the animals then lived, I always heard that sound as anguish. It held no defiance or nobility—just pain. But I'd be overstating it to suggest that some thirty years later the memory of caged lions calling across the water had somehow drawn me back to this project. At least, not consciously.

Essentially I'm a portrait photographer. Earning a living means that I'm predominantly a hired gun. These days almost no one has their picture taken for the sake of it. The end use of the images in advertising or magazines, on posters or album covers means that the portrait is doing a job. Its main purpose is to sell; to make the subject look more beautiful, interesting or sexy than they really are. Phyllis Diller once said, 'My photographs do me an injustice. They look just like me.' There's not much danger of that any more.

Ich kann nicht behaupten, daß ich über eine besondere Beziehung zu Tieren verfüge. Als Asthmatiker darf ich noch nicht einmal einen Hund oder eine Katze halten, und auf mein Verhältnis zum Wellensittich meiner Tochter wäre Prof. Grzimek auch nicht gerade stolz. Als Kind ging ich vielleicht zweimal im Jahr in den Zoo von Taronga. Meine Mutter besitzt ein Foto aus den fünfziger Jahren, das mich mit einem weißen Kaninchen im Arm im Zoo zeigt. An die Tiere kann ich mich nicht erinnern — aber den Boxkampf mit meinem Vetter Wilfred am gleichen Tag habe ich nicht vergessen. Ich gewann.

Ich wuchs im Double Bay-Viertel von Sydney auf; damals war dieser Stadtteil noch nicht Wohnort der gelifteten Designershop-Schickeria, die drei Autos pro Haushalt besitzt. Meine Mutter hatte zu Hause ein kleines Wettbüro, und manchmal mußte ich die Wetten annehmen. Wenn in den Sommernächten der Nordwestwind blies, kam es vor, daß ich in meinem Bett lag und seltsame, gespenstische Geräusche hörte, die über den Hafen wehten. Es war das Gebrüll der Löwen, die im Zoo in ihren traurigen Betongruben gefangen saßen. Da ich wußte, unter welchen Bedingungen sie und viele andere Tiere zu dieser Zeit leben mußten, habe ich dieses Gebrüll immer als Ausdruck der Qual empfunden. Es enthielt weder Trotz noch Würde — nur Schmerz. Es wäre aber übertrieben zu behaupten, daß die Erinnerung an eingesperrte Löwen, die mich über das Wasser riefen, der Auslöser für dieses Projekt gewesen wäre — zumindest nicht bewußt.

Eigentlich bin ich Porträtfotograf. Da ich damit meinen Lebensunterhalt verdienen muß, arbeite ich hauptsächlich als eine Art Söldner. Heutzutage läßt sich kaum noch jemand zu seinem Vergnügen fotografieren. Ein Bild in der Werbung oder in einem Magazin, auf einem Poster oder Plattencover erfüllt einen bestimmten Zweck — es muß verkaufen und ein Objekt schöner, interessanter oder aufregender aussehen lassen, als es wirklich ist. Phyllis Diller hat einmal gesagt: »Meine Fotos tun mir unrecht. Sie sehen genauso aus wie ich.« Diese Gefahr besteht heute kaum noch.

Je ne revendique aucune affinité particulière avec les animaux. L'asthme m'empêche de posséder un chien ou un chat et, mes relations avec la perruche de ma fille n'ont jamais véritablement menacé le Dr Doolittle. Quand j'étais enfant, on m'emmenait environ deux fois par an au zoo de Taronga. Ma mère possède une photographie datant des années 50 me représentant au zoo tenant dans les bras un lapin. Je n'ai aucun souvenir des animaux — ce dont je me rappelle avec le plus d'acuité, c'est que ce jour-là je me suis bagarré avec mon cousin Wilfred, et que je l'ai battu.

J'ai grandi à Sydney, sur les rives de Double Bay. A l'époque, ce n'était pas encore l'abreuvoir des foules liftées, dotées de pavillons avec trois garages et nées pour le shopping que ce quartier est devenu aujourd'hui. Maman faisait à l'occasion office de bookmaker à la maison, et parfois je prenais les paris. Les soirs d'été, quand soufflait le vent du nord-ouest, on pouvait entendre, allongé dans son lit, un son étrange et obsédant flotter sur le port. C'était le rugissement des lions du zoo qui montait de leurs tristes fosses en béton. Probablement parce que je connaissais leurs conditions d'existence, ainsi que celles de bien d'autres animaux, j'ai toujours associé ce son à l'angoisse. Il n'avait rien du défi ou de la noblesse — ce n'était que souffrance. Il serait toutefois exagéré d'insinuer que quelque trente ans plus tard, ce serait le souvenir de l'appel des lions encagés me parvenant par dessus les eaux du port qui m'aurait en quelque sorte fait revenir pour réaliser ce projet. Du moins, pas consciemment.

Je suis pour l'essentiel un portraitiste et, si je souhaite pouvoir vivre de ma photographie, foncièrement un mercenaire. Presque plus personne ne se fait photographier aujourd'hui pour l'amour de l'art. L'image ayant pour finalité la publicité ou le magazine, l'affiche, la couverture de livre ou de disque, le portrait remplit une fonction économique précise. Son objectif principal, c'est de faire vendre, de montrer le sujet plus beau, plus intéressant ou plus sexy qu'il ne l'est en réalité. Si Phyllis Diller a pu dire jadis : « Mes photographies sont injustes à mon égard : elles me ressemblent », on ne risque aujourd'hui plus guère de courir un tel danger.

While one must still employ one's range of techniques to get the shot, the commercial realities reduce the chances of producing something surprising, dangerous or subversive. Instead of being journeys of discovery they're more often package tours to Las Vegas where you could still win the jackpot but it's unlikely.

So from time to time one feels the need to throw away the map and go looking for adventure. My previous exhibition was a collection of nudes—men and women. Much of my work in Australia and the United States has been with celebrities. I've photographed people like Madonna, George Burns, Frank Zappa, Judy Davis, Andy Warhol and Joe Cocker—every one of them a photographic pussycat compared to the animals in this collection.

Portrait photography is a curious craft. Even when you're delivering to a specific brief it can involve an intimacy between photographer and subject that would normally take forever. In an hour or two you have to convince a total stranger, if not to trust you, then to share a few secrets and expose some essence of who they are—or think they are.

Part of the portrait photographer's job is to break down and through the subject's natural resistance. As a result, we can end up with a bag of personality tricks. There are still some photographers who use variations of the 'give-it-to-me-baby' *Blow-Up* approach to the subject. But generally it's a matter of different strokes... Getting subjects to overcome their reticence and stop them trying to hide in the corners of their face, their body or the studio demands a rapid psychological assessment and an appropriate performance. Accordingly, you run the gamut from bully to sycophant, Joe Cool to simpatico hustler. You can

---

Der technische Aufwand für eine Aufnahme ist gleich geblieben, aber durch die kommerziellen Zwänge sind die Chancen auf ein überraschendes, gefährliches oder gar subversives Foto erheblich gesunken. Fotos sind heute keine Entdeckungsreise mehr, sondern eher eine Pauschalreise nach Las Vegas: Man kann zwar immer noch den Jackpot gewinnen, aber es ist sehr, sehr unwahrscheinlich.

So überkommt einen von Zeit zu Zeit die Lust, alle Landkarten wegzuwerfen und das Abenteuer zu suchen. Meine letzte Fotoausstellung war eine Reihe von Akten — von Männern und Frauen. In Australien und den Vereinigten Staaten habe ich häufig mit Stars zusammengearbeitet. Ich habe Madonna, George Burns, Frank Zappa, Judy Davis, Andy Warhol und Joe Cocker fotografiert — jeder von ihnen war ein zahmes Schmusekätzchen im Vergleich zu den Tieren in dieser Reihe.

Die Porträtfotografie ist ein eigenartiges Handwerk. Selbst wenn man ganz bestimmte Vorgaben zu erfüllen hat, kann dabei ein intimes Verhältnis zwischen Modell und Fotograf entstehen — eine Entwicklung, die normalerweise Jahre brauchen würde. In ein oder zwei Stunden muß der Fotograf einen völlig Fremden davon überzeugen, Vertrauen zu fassen, einige Geheimnisse preiszugeben und etwas von seinem wahren Ich zu enthüllen — oder von dem, was er oder sie dafür hält.

Ein Teil der Aufgabe eines Porträtfotografen besteht darin, die natürlichen Schutzmauern seines Modells niederzureißen oder zu durchbrechen. Daher lernt man im Laufe der Zeit einen ganzen Haufen von Tricks. Es gibt immer noch Fotografen, die mit Variationen der »Zeigs mir, Baby«-*Blow-Up*-Masche an ihr Modell herangehen. Aber im allgemeinen ist das Ganze eine Frage von Zuckerbrot und Peitsche... Ein Modell dazu zu bewegen, seine Zurückhaltung abzulegen und sich nicht mehr in den Ecken des eigenen Gesichts, des Körpers oder des Studios zu verstecken, erfordert eine schnelle psychologische Auffassungsgabe und die angemessene Verhaltensweise. Dementsprechend muß der Fotograf alle Register ziehen — vom Grobian bis zum Speichellecker, von

---

Tandis qu'il est toujours nécessaire de maîtriser tout un éventail de techniques personnelles pour obtenir la photo, les réalités commerciales limitent les occasions de produire quelque chose de surprenant, de dangereux, voire de subversif. Plutôt qu'à l'aventure, cela ressemble le plus souvent à un voyage organisé à Las Vegas, où si l'on peut toujours remporter le gros lot cela demeure très improbable.

C'est pourquoi, l'envie vous prend parfois de jeter la carte aux orties et de partir à l'aventure. Mon exposition précédente avait pour thème le nu — masculin et féminin. En Australie et aux Etats-Unis, j'ai réalisé l'essentiel de mon travail avec des célébrités. J'ai photographié des personnalités comme Madonna, George Burns, Frank Zappa, Judy Davis, Andy Warhol et Joe Cocker, qui étaient tous des agneaux comparés aux animaux photographiés dans cet ouvrage.

Le portrait photographique est un métier bien singulier. Même si le délai de livraison est impératif, il peut impliquer une intimité entre le photographe et son sujet qui, en temps normal, aurait demandé des années. En moins d'une heure ou deux, il faut convaincre un étranger sinon de vous faire confiance, du moins de partager avec vous quelques secrets, de lever le voile sur l'essence de ce qu'il est, ou de ce qu'il pense être.

Puisque le travail du photographe portraitiste consiste en partie à surmonter la résistance naturelle du sujet, on en vient à mettre en œuvre tout un arsenal de ficelles du métier. En ce qui concerne l'approche du sujet, certains photographes utilisent encore diverses variations sur le thème du « C'est bon, coco » façon *Blow-Up*. Cependant, en général, tout est une question de feeling... Parvenir à obtenir du sujet qu'il surmonte ses réticences, qu'il cesse d'essayer de se cacher dans les recoins de son visage, de son corps ou du studio exige une rapide évaluation psychologique et un comportement adéquat. Par conséquent, on passe par toute une gamme d'attitudes, du tyran au flagorneur, du pépère au débrouillard sympathique. On cajole, on câline et séduit, on

cajole, wheedle and seduce, relax, confront and inspire. Sometimes you can simply be yourself—if you can remember what that is. But when it comes to photographing animals, anything you've ever learnt about motivating human subjects is utterly useless.

To complete this confession I have two further revelations: I didn't know what I was up against when I decided to pursue this project, and I am not a patient man. In this case, when I threw away the map I had no idea quite how much trouble I was going looking for. I was, at least, trying something that I had never seen done before and in answer to William Blake's poetic question, 'What immortal hand or eye could frame thy fearful symmetry?', I somewhat arrogantly said, 'Mine!'

Of course, it wasn't to be undertaken in any forests of the night. That fact lured me into my first false assumption. Because I'd be working with zoo animals—creatures who were used to contact with the visiting public, their keepers, vets and zoo staff—I began with an expectation that the animals would be, to some degree, open to manipulation. With a little persistence and the encouragement of food dropped in the right place, I believed that they'd eventually be in a position to give me a shot.

While not exclusively so, eye-contact with the lens is a major element of portraiture. Even if the idea of the eyes being windows to the soul has been overstated, tradition and social conditioning demands we look each other in the eye. The fact that it's the skin, flesh and muscle movement—not the eye itself—that communicates or tries to disguise, makes no difference. We expect to see the eyes and, ideally, both of them.

Joe Cool bis zum Mann für alle Fälle. Man kann jemandem gut zureden, ihn oder sie umschmeicheln und verführen, entpannen, mit etwas konfrontieren oder inspirieren. Manchmal darf der Fotograf auch einfach er selbst sein — wenn er sich noch daran erinnert, wer er ist. Aber wenn es um Tieraufnahmen geht, sind alle Tricks, die man jemals zur Motivation menschlicher Modelle angewandt hat, absolut nutzlos.

Der Vollständigkeit halber muß ich noch zwei weitere Dinge beichten: Ich hatte keine Ahnung, was auf mich zukam, als ich mit diesem Projekt begann, und ich bin kein sehr geduldiger Mensch. Als ich also diesmal meine Landkarte wegwarf, wußte ich nicht, welche Schwierigkeiten mich erwarteten. Immerhin versuchte ich etwas, das ich noch nie zuvor ausprobiert hatte, und antwortete auf William Blakes poetische Frage »Welche unsterbliche Hand, welches Auge konnten dein furchtbares Ebenmaß fügen?« mit einem einigermaßen arroganten: »Meine!«.

Natürlich sollte das Ganze nicht mitten in der Nacht in irgendwelchen Wäldern stattfinden, und diese Tatsache verleitete mich zu meiner ersten Fehleinschätzung. Da ich mit Zootieren arbeiten wollte — Tiere, die den Kontakt mit Besuchern, Pflegern, Tierärzten und Zoopersonal gewohnt waren —, ging ich an die Aufgabe in der Erwartung heran, daß die Tiere in einem gewissen Maß manipulierbar seien. Ich war mir sicher, daß sie sich — mit ein wenig Ausdauer meinerseits und Ermutigungen in Form von Nahrung an der richtigen Stelle — für ein paar Aufnahmen in die richtige Position bringen lassen würden.

Trotz einiger Ausnahmen gehört der Augenkontakt mit der Linse zu den wichtigsten Elementen der Porträtfotografie. Auch wenn die Behauptung, daß die Augen das Fenster zur menschlichen Seele darstellen, leicht übertrieben ist, verlangen Tradition und soziale Normen, daß wir einander in die Augen schauen. Dabei spielt es keine Rolle, daß es nicht das Auge selbst, sondern eigentlich die Haut, das Fleisch und die Bewegung der Muskeln sind, die kommunizieren oder etwas zu verbergen versuchen. Wir wollen unserem Gegenüber ins Auge blicken — und möglichst in beide.

détend, affronte et inspire. Parfois, il suffit d'être soi-même — si l'on parvient à s'en souvenir! Mais quand il s'agit de photographier des animaux, tout ce que l'on a pu apprendre sur la motivation des sujets humains se révèle inutile.

Pour parachever cette confession, il me reste deux révélations à faire : je ne savais pas ce qui m'attendait quand j'ai décidé d'entreprendre ce projet, et la patience n'est pas une de mes principales caractéristiques. Dans ces conditions, lorsque j'ai jeté la carte aux orties, je n'avais pas la moindre idée des difficultés que j'allais rencontrer. J'essayais, du moins, de faire quelque chose qui, à ma connaissance, n'avait jamais été réalisé et, en réponse à la question du poète William Blake : « Quelle main ou quel œil immortels sauront saisir ton effrayante symétrie ? », j'affirmai avec une arrogance certaine : « Moi ! »

Naturellement, il était hors de question de réaliser ceci dans quelque forêt obscure. Ceci m'induisit à formuler une première hypothèse erronée. En raison du fait que je travaillerais dans un zoo — c'est-à-dire avec des animaux habitués à fréquenter le public, leurs gardiens, leurs vétérinaires et le personnel de l'établissement — j'avais l'espoir que les bêtes seraient, dans une certaine mesure, enclines à la manipulation. Avec un peu de persévérance et l'encouragement d'un peu de nourriture lancé au bon endroit, je croyais qu'elles finiraient par se mettre en position de me donner une bonne photographie.

Bien qu'il n'en soit pas toujours exclusivement ainsi, la relation yeux-objectif constitue un élément fondamental du portrait. Même si l'idée selon laquelle les yeux sont une fenêtre ouverte sur l'âme a été exagérée, la tradition et le conditionnement social exigent que nous regardions l'autre dans les yeux. Que ce soient la peau, la chair ainsi que le mouvement des muscles — et non l'œil même — qui communiquent ou tentent de masquer ne fait aucune différence. Nous nous attendons à voir les yeux et, idéalement, les deux.

L'autre élément que j'avais choisi d'utiliser, c'est le classique fond uni, noir ou blanc. (A notre époque de l'électronique triomphante, j'aurais pu me contenter de supprimer les arrière-plans grâce à l'ordinateur, mais cette solution ne me paraissait pas la bonne, quoique ici le désespoir m'y ait quelques fois

The other element that I'd chosen to use was the classic flat background, black or white. (In this electronic age I could have stripped in the backgrounds on computer, but that didn't seem right, even though there are a couple of shots in the collection where desperation has forced me to do it.) You need a lot of canvas to backdrop an elephant or a giraffe, and in all cases I'd be introducing a new, alien element to the animals' familiar environment, so I knew from the start that there would be difficulties.

Curiosity, anger, disdain, avoidance and destruction were just some of the responses the canvas intruders provoked. Large backdrops became smaller ones as rhino, hippo and lion turned on them with savage delight and territorial vengeance. The fact that sometimes the canvas came with the scent of the last animal to be photographed didn't help. 'I'm not going near that bloody thing' was a common reaction.

Sometimes it wasn't aggro towards the canvas that made a shot impossible—it was a total obsession with it. The animal would stand steadfastly eyeing the background invader for an eternity—a bum-to-camera game of whoever blinks first loses. Occasionally they'd become besotted with it, grunting and snuffling over it in an endless love. The attitude to the backdrop was never predictable.

The emu went into a beady-eyed trance when it saw the thing and it'd probably still be standing there practising its thousand-yard stare, just out of shot, if we didn't simply manhandle the bird into position. It wasn't that easy with a lot of them. Just when I thought I'd worked it out and planned accordingly, the rules would change.

The fruit bat was happy to hang there, perfectly positioned, but I wanted it to spread its wings to get the Batman shadow on the backdrop. Finally, two hours later it obliged. My victories of manipulation were generally minor ones: the artful crossover curves in the shot of the Rainforest Dragons were, I confess,

---

Ein weiterer Bestandteil dieser Serie sollte der klassische glatte Hintergrund in Schwarz oder Weiß sein. (In unserem Elektronikzeitalter hätte ich natürlich die realen Hintergründe mit Hilfe des Computers entfernen können, aber das erschien mir falsch. Allerdings gibt es einige Fotos in diesem Band, bei denen mich die Verzweiflung zwang, so vorzugehen.) Für einen Elefanten oder eine Giraffe benötigt man eine Menge Leinwand als Hintergrund, und in allen Fällen brachte ich damit ein neues, fremdartiges Element in die vertraute Umgebung der Tiere — also konnte ich davon ausgehen, daß es Schwierigkeiten geben würde.

Neugier, Zorn, Verachtung, Distanz und Zerstörung waren nur einige der Reaktionen, die wir Eindringlinge mit der Leinwand provozierten. Große Hintergründe wurden kleiner, wenn sich Nashorn, Nilpferd und Löwe ihnen mit rohem Vergnügen und territorialer Rachelust widmeten. Und die Tatsache, daß die Leinwand manchmal noch den Geruch des zuletzt portraitierten Tieres trug, machte die Sache auch nicht einfacher. »Ich stelle mich nicht vor das verdammte Ding« war eine häufig zu beobachtende Reaktion.

Manchmal machte jedoch nicht die Aggression gegen die Leinwand ein Foto unmöglich — sondern die völlige Fixierung darauf. In solchen Fällen stand das Tier für eine halbe Ewigkeit mit dem Rücken zur Kamera und starrte unerschütterlich auf den Eindringling im Hintergrund — das alte Hintern-zur-Kamera-Spiel: Wer zuerst blinzelt, hat verloren. Manche Tiere waren völlig vernarrt in die Leinwand, begannen zu grunzen und beschnüffelten sie mit unendlicher Liebe. Die Reaktionen auf den Hintergrund ließen sich unmöglich vorhersagen.

Der Emu verfiel in eine perläugige Trance, als er das »Ding« sah, und er würde wahrscheinlich noch heute dort stehen und sein Tausend-Meter-Starren üben — knapp außerhalb der Reichweite der Kamera —, wenn wir ihn nicht in die richtige Position getragen hätten. Mit vielen anderen Tieren war es nicht so einfach. Immer, wenn ich dachte, daß ich das Spiel durchschaut hätte und dementsprechend vorausplante, änderten sich die Regeln.

---

contraint.) Il faut un métrage de tissu considérable pour placer un éléphant ou une girafe sur une toile de fond, sans parler du fait que j'introduisais ainsi un objet aussi nouveau qu'étranger dans l'environnement familier de l'animal, aussi savais-je dès le départ que les difficultés ne manqueraient pas.

Curiosité, colère, mépris, évitement et destruction, telles furent quelques-unes des réactions provoquées par l'intrusion de la toile de fond. Les toiles de fond de grand format s'amenuisaient rapidement à mesure que rhinocéros, hippopotame et lion s'y attaquaient avec une joie sauvage dictée par leur instinct de vengeance territoriale. Que la toile ait été parfois encore imprégnée de l'odeur de l'animal précédemment photographié n'arrangeait certainement pas les choses. « Je ne vais pas me rapprocher de ce truc » était une attitude courante.

Quelquefois, ce n'était pas l'agressivité envers la toile de fond qui rendait impossible la prise de vue, c'était l'obsession. L'animal, statufié, contemplait inébranlablement l'intrus durant une éternité, comme dans un jeu d'arrière-train face à l'objectif où le premier qui bronchait avait perdu. Parfois, il s'en éprenait, grognant autour d'elle et la flairant, lui vouant un amour éternel. L'attitude des animaux envers la toile de fond n'était jamais prévisible.

Quand il vit la chose, l'émeu entra en transe : il serait probablement toujours là, ses yeux en perles plongés dans une contemplation séculaire, hors du cadre, si nous n'avions pas tout simplement déplacé nous-mêmes l'oiseau à la force des bras. Mais pour nombre d'animaux, ce ne fut pas aussi simple. Quand je pensais avoir compris et planifiais en conséquence la prise de vue, les règles du jeu changeaient.

La roussette semblait très heureuse d'être accrochée ici, parfaitement positionnée, mais je voulais qu'elle déploie ses ailes afin d'obtenir une ombre façon Batman sur la toile de fond. Finalement, deux heures plus tard, elle obtempéra. Mes victoires en termes de manipulation étaient en général bien maigres : les artistiques courbes entrecroisées des varans de la forêt tropicale ont été obtenues, je dois l'avouer, en modifiant à l'aide d'un crayon la disposition de leurs queues. Le cacatoès n'a exhibé fort opportunément sa crête soufrée qu'à l'instant où on lui a présenté un grand lézard.

achieved by using a pencil to rearrange their tails. The fact that the cockatoo accommodatingly flared its sulphur crest was the result of showing it a big lizard at the critical moment.

With the echidna shot I was determined to see its tongue. It was equally determined to play spiky football till hell froze over, if that was how long it would take for me to give up. Thanks to a keeper and an irresistible—to echidnas—mess of pottage, it finally surrendered a moment of its soul and tongue.

My initial aim with this book was to capture on film the greatest variety of animals possible. After two years, 110 individual animals and 600 rolls of film—ten shots to the roll—I've been forced to admit defeat with many of them. Some because the shots simply weren't good enough; others because the subjects just wouldn't 'behave' for the camera.

At the heart of this practical difficulty is the truism that these wild animals are wild. Only the seals at Taronga earn their keep by performing for the public. The others aren't tame, and it hardly needs to be said that the wilder we keep them the better. I have the greatest admiration for the people and the principles behind both Taronga and Western Plains Zoos. Their policy is to modify the animals' behaviour to the absolute practicable minimum and to recreate for them, as far as possible, their natural habitat.

Although initially I felt uneasy about zoos and the justification behind keeping animals in captivity, I now have no such compunction about places like Taronga Park and Western Plains. These zoos operate like a gene-bank for endangered species and allow us to make the acquaintance of these animals, at

Die Fledermaus hing gerne vor meiner Kamera, in der perfekten Position. Aber ich wollte, daß sie ihre Flügel spreizte, um den Batman-Schatten auf den Hintergund zu bekommen — und zwei Stunden später tat sie mir den Gefallen. Erfolgreiche Manipulationen gelangen mir nur äußerst selten: Die Aufnahme der kunstvoll gekreuzten Schwänze der Hypsilurus spinipes entstand — ich muß es zugeben — mit Hilfe eines Bleistifts, und der Gelbhauben-Kakadu spreizte seinen gelben Kopfschmuck nur deshalb so bereitwillig, weil wir ihm im richtigen Augenblick eine große Echse zeigten.

Auf dem Foto des Australischen Ameisenigels wollte ich unbedingt seine Zunge zeigen. Er dagegen war genauso fest entschlossen, bis ans Ende aller Zeiten Nadelkissen zu spielen — und auch noch länger, wenn es so lange dauern sollte, bis ich aufgab. Dank eines Pflegers und einer — für Ameisenigel — unwiderstehlichen Portion Gemüsepampe mit Fleisch ließ mich das Tier einen Augenblick in seine Seele und auf seine Zunge blicken.

Ursprünglich wollte ich für dieses Buch die größtmögliche Anzahl von Tieren fotografieren. Aber nach zwei Jahren, 110 Tieren und 600 Rollen Film — mit zehn Fotos pro Rolle — mußte ich meine Niederlage im Kampf mit vielen von ihnen eingestehen: Manchmal waren die Fotos einfach nicht gut genug, aber teilweise lag es auch daran, daß sich die Modelle vor der Kamera einfach nicht »benehmen« wollten.

Die Gründe für diese Schwierigkeiten in der Praxis können in dem Gemeinplatz zusammengefaßt werden, daß wilde Tiere wirklich wild sind. Nur die Seehunde im Zoo von Taronga verdienen ihren Lebensunterhalt mit Auftritten vor Publikum. Die anderen Tiere sind nicht zahm, und es muß eigentlich nicht erwähnt werden, daß man sie auch so wild wie möglich halten sollte. Ich empfinde größte Hochachtung für die Menschen und die Prinzipien in den Zoos von Taronga und Western Plains, die Veränderungen im Verhalten der Tiere nur auf ein absolutes Minimum beschränken und so weit wie möglich einen natürlichen Lebensraum für sie schaffen.

Trotz meiner anfänglichen Bedenken gegen zoologische Gärten und die Begründungen für eine Tierhaltung in Gefangenschaft empfinde ich an Orten wie Taronga und Western Plains keine derartigen Gewissensbisse. Diese Zoos funktionieren wie eine Gen-Bank für gefährdete Tierarten und ermöglichen uns, die Tiere

Quant à la photo de l'échidné, j'étais déterminé à voir sa langue. Celui-ci était tout autant déterminé à imiter quelque ballon de football épineux jusqu'à ce que gèle l'enfer, si c'était le temps qu'il me fallait pour abandonner. Grâce à un gardien ainsi qu'à un brouet de légumes et de viande irrésistible — pour les échidnés — , il baissa un instant sa garde, me laissant photographier et son âme et sa langue.

L'objectif initial de ce livre était de saisir sur la pellicule la plus grande diversité d'animaux possible. Après deux ans de travail, 110 animaux et 600 rouleaux de film (à raison de dix poses par rouleau), j'ai été contraint d'admettre ma défaite face à maints d'entre eux. Parfois, tout simplement parce que les clichés n'étaient pas bons, parfois parce que le sujet ne voulait pas « poser » devant l'appareil photo.

Au cœur de cette difficulté pratique réside une lapalissade : ces animaux sauvages sont sauvages. A Taronga, seuls les phoques gagnent leur subsistance en se donnant en spectacle au public. Les autres ne sont pas apprivoisés, et il n'est guère utile de préciser que plus nous nous efforcerons de préserver leur caractère sauvage, mieux cela vaudra. J'éprouve l'admiration la plus vive pour le personnel et les principes qui soutiennent les zoos de Taronga et de Western Plains. Leur politique consiste à ne modifier le comportement des animaux qu'en tout dernier recours et le moins possible, ainsi qu'à recréer, autant que faire se peut, leur habitat naturel.

Bien qu'à l'origine les zoos et les justifications avancées pour garder des animaux en captivité me mettaient mal à l'aise, je n'ai désormais plus aucun scrupule de la sorte envers des établissements comme ceux de Taronga Park et de Western Plains. Ces zoos, qui font office de banques de gènes pour les espèces en voie d'extinction, nous permettent de connaître ces animaux, tout en nous faisant prendre conscience de leur triste sort et en nous incitant à agir pour assurer leur survie. Le programme d'élevage des rhinocéros noirs, espèce quasiment éteinte, mis en œuvre à Western Plains n'est rien moins qu'héroïque, et le dévouement prodigué par le personnel méconnu du zoo est tout aussi édifiant qu'il inspire l'humilité.

the same time making us aware of their plight and moving us to take action to ensure their survival. The Western Plains' programme to breed black rhinos back from the brink is nothing less than heroic and the level of dedication among the unsung zoo staff is both inspirational and humbling.

Even though the animals I encountered were damned if they were going to make it easy for me, the images in this book tend to tame them and present them for public consumption. I can't deny a degree of the cutefactor in some of the shots, as well as in their selection. But how else, for example, can you photograph the baby tiger? During the two years I worked on the book, I continually questioned whether my photographs would have any role in the survival of these creatures, and came increasingly to feel that they carry an implication that is more important than whether they merely engage the eye. Look at the photograph of the koala. It's virtually impossible to make a koala look anything but appealing. At least as much as the kangaroo, the koala is the great Australian icon. It allows the world to see us, perhaps falsely, as a better nation than we are. Any people who inhabit a land in which these creatures live can't be all bad. Yet we go on destroying their habitat and therefore their future in the name of development.

They tell a story at Taronga about a man in the 1930s who for some strange reason stole a couple of cassowary eggs from the zoo. For his trouble he was severely slashed by the broody bird's clawed feet. Bleeding, he carried the stolen eggs on to the ferry and by the time he'd reached Circular Quay he'd bled to death.

The temptation to rejoice in the morality of this tale is tempered by the fact that in the Daintree Rainforest today the cassowary is almost certainly doomed, its numbers diminishing towards extinction. There are road signs pleading with you to drive carefully through the Daintree in case you bowl a

---

kennenzulernen, während sie uns gleichzeitig auf deren Notlage aufmerksam machen und uns um Beistand im Kampf um deren Überleben bitten. Das Western Plains-Programm zur Züchtung der vom Aussterben bedrohten Spitzmaulnashörner ist ein heroischer Versuch, und die Hingabe des selten gewürdigten Zoopersonals wirkt inspirierend und demütigend zugleich.

Obwohl die Tiere, denen ich begegnete, es mir alles andere als leicht machten, lassen die Fotos in diesem Buch sie zahm und für den Umgang mit Menschen geeignet erscheinen. Natürlich kann ich einigen Aufnahmen eine gewisse niedliche Ausstrahlung nicht absprechen — aber wie soll man beispielsweise ein Tigerbaby sonst fotografieren? In den zwei Jahren, in denen ich an diesem Buch arbeitete, habe ich mich immer wieder gefragt, ob meine Fotos für das Überleben dieser Kreaturen irgendeine Rolle spielen werden. Dabei gelangte ich mehr und mehr zu der Überzeugung, daß diese Bilder eine tiefe innere Bedeutung in sich tragen, die wichtiger ist als die Frage, ob sie das Auge erfreuen oder nicht. Ein gutes Beispiel sind die Aufnahmen des Koalabären: Es ist praktisch unmöglich, ihn anders als anziehend aussehen zu lassen. Und mindestens so sehr wie das Känguruh gilt der Koalabär als das Wahrzeichen Australiens. Dank seiner Hilfe hält die Welt uns, vielleicht zu Unrecht, für eine bessere Nation, als wir in Wahrheit sind — denn die Menschen, die ein Land bewohnen, in dem solche Tiere leben, können einfach nicht schlecht sein. Dennoch zerstören wir im Namen des Fortschritts den Lebensraum der Koalas und damit ihre Zukunft.

In Taronga erzählt man die Geschichte von einem Mann, der in den 30er Jahren aus irgendeinem abwegigen Grund einige Kasuar-Eier aus dem Zoo stahl. Dabei trat ihn der brütende Vogel mit seinen Klauenfüßen und verletzte ihn schwer. Blutend schleppte der Mann die gestohlenen Eier zur Fähre, und als das Boot Circular Quay erreichte, war er bereits verblutet.

Die Versuchung, sich an der Moral von der Geschichte zu erfreuen, wird im Keim erstickt durch die Tatsache, daß der Kasuar in den Regenwäldern von Daintree heute kurz vor dem Aussterben steht. Man findet dort Straßenschilder, die Autofahrer bitten, vorsichtig zu fahren, damit kein Kasuar über-

---

Même si les animaux que j'y ai rencontrés se seraient damnés pour ne pas me faciliter le travail, les images composant cet ouvrage tendent à les apprivoiser, à les offrir à la consommation du public. Je ne saurais nier une certaine malice dans quelques-unes des prises de vue ainsi que dans leur choix, mais comment, par exemple, pourrait-on photographier différemment le bébé tigre ? Au cours de ces deux années de travail, je ne cessais de me demander si mes photographies pourraient jouer un rôle quelconque dans la survie de ces créatures, et vins à penser avec toujours davantage de conviction qu'elles avaient une signification bien plus importante que le simple fait de savoir si elles plairaient. Prenez la photographie du koala. Il est quasiment impossible de montrer un koala autrement que séduisant. Au moins autant que le kangourou, c'est le symbole de l'Australie, grâce auquel le monde nous voit, probablement à tort, comme une nation meilleure que nous ne le sommes. Quelqu'un qui habite un pays où vivent de telles créatures ne peut être entièrement mauvais. Pourtant, nous continuons à détruire leur habitat, et donc leur avenir, au nom du progrès.

On raconte à Taronga l'histoire d'un homme qui, dans les années 30, vola pour une raison mystérieuse deux œufs de casoar au zoo. Gravement griffé d'un coup de patte par l'oiseau couveur et perdant son sang, il transporta les œufs jusqu'au ferry ; avant d'atteindre Circular Quay il avait succombé à une hémorragie.

L'envie de se réjouir de la morale de cette histoire est tempérée par le fait que, dans la forêt tropicale de Daintree, le casoar est aujourd'hui presque certainement condamné, sa population s'amenuisant inéluctablement. Dans cette forêt, des panneaux de signalisation invitent l'automobiliste à rouler prudemment, afin de ne pas renverser un casoar qui traverserait la route, impliquant par là que ce serait la faute du conducteur. De fait, c'est le percement de la route à travers la région de Daintree, pour complaire aux exigences du touriste et de ses dollars, qui a scellé le destin du casoar.

C'eût été un acte de foi que de voir figurer ici le casoar. Malheureusement, en dépit de trois tentatives, j'ai échoué. Je ne suis jamais parvenu à obtenir une prise de vue de qualité. C'est pourquoi seuls les mots exprimeront mon hommage envers ce grand oiseau qui se défendit naguère seulement pour

cassowary. The implication is that it's your fault when, in fact, sealing the road through the rainforest to leech the tourist dollar and all it demands, sealed the fate of the cassowary.

It was an act of faith that the cassowary would feature here. But despite three attempts, I failed. I never got a quality shot. So words have to carry my tribute to a big bird that once fought back only to perish at the hands of a dumb political and economic greed that is not uniquely Queensland's. In a way the road signs' implication is right. We are all co-conspirators in the demise of the cassowary.

It's also difficult not to approve of the female African elephant Yum Yum's less dramatic retort some years ago to a particular biker. He and his mates, as was then the practice, had been feeding her the yellow-flowered plants that grew near the enclosure. On being offered one of the plants Yum Yum held it close to her eye to check that it was the right stuff. The biker sneered at her, calling her a 'blind bitch'. She took herself and her feelings off to the mudpool, returned a few minutes later, singled out the loudmouth, and doused him with a trunkload of foul-smelling mud. It could have been worse. Yum Yum is the lady who shared with us her undoubtedly successful attempt on the *Guinness Book of Records* magnitude and duration mark for wind-breaking.

It's harder to know what to feel about Congo, the male African elephant at Western Plains. He began his public career as the baby in the film *Hatari!* You start off working with John Wayne and Howard Hawks, Henry Mancini composes 'Baby Elephant Walk'

---

fahren wird. Auf diese Weise soll impliziert werden, daß die Ausrottung des Kasuars die Schuld des jeweiligen unglücklichen Autofahrers ist; dabei war sein Schicksal bereits besiegelt, als man die Straße durch den Regenwald baute, um den Touristen die Dollars noch besser aus der Tasche ziehen zu können.

Mein großes Ziel war, den Kasuar in den Mittelpunkt des Buches zu stellen. Aber trotz dreier Versuche habe ich versagt: Es gelang mir nicht, auch nur eine einzige vernünftige Aufnahme zu machen. Deshalb müssen Worte meine Hochachtung vor einem großen Vogel ausdrücken, der einst zurückschlug, nur um an dummer, kurzsichtiger politischer und wirtschaftlicher Habgier zugrunde zu gehen, wie man sie nicht nur in Queensland findet. In einer Hinsicht trifft die Implikation des Straßenschilds zu: Wir sind alle mitverantwortlich für das Ende der Kasuare.

Für die etwas weniger dramatische Reaktion der Afrikanischen Elefantenkuh Yum Yum auf einen bestimmten Motorradfahrer kann man vollstes Verständnis haben. Er und seine Freunde hatten sie, wie damals üblich, mit den gelbblütigen Pflanzen gefüttert, die in der Nähe der Umzäunung wuchsen. Als Yum Yum eine dieser Pflanzen angeboten bekam, hielt sie sie vor ihr Auge, um zu prüfen, ob es sich um die richtige Sorte handelte. Der Motorradfahrer lachte sie aus und nannte sie eine »blinde Kuh«. Daraufhin zog sie sich mit ihren verletzten Gefühlen in ein Schlammloch zurück, kam einige Minuten später wieder an den Zaun, suchte und fand das Großmaul und übergoß ihn mit einem Rüssel voll faulig riechenden Schlamms. Es hätte schlimmer kommen können: Yum Yum ist die Dame, bei deren zweifellos erfolgreichem Versuch, mit einem Furz ungeahnter Stärke und Dauer ins *Guinness Buch der Rekorde* zu gelangen, wir Zeuge sein durften.

Bei Congo, dem Afrikanischen Elefanten in Western Plains, ist es dagegen schwieriger, mit seinen Gefühlen ins Reine zu kommen. Congo begann seine Karriere als Elefantenbaby im Film *Hatari!* Da arbeiten Sie mit John Wayne und Howard Hawks, Henry Mancini komponiert für Sie »Baby Elephant Walk« — und dreiunddreißig Jahre später leben Sie in Dubbo im Zoo.

---

succomber sous les assauts de la cupidité politique et économique qui n'est pas exclusivement celle du Queensland. Le sous-entendu des panneaux de signalisation est, en un sens, exact. Nous avons tous comploté la mort du casoar.

Il est également difficile de ne pas approuver la riposte, moins dramatique, que fit voici quelques années Yum Yum, un éléphant femelle d'Afrique, à un motard. Comme c'était l'habitude à l'époque, celui-ci, en compagnie de ses camarades, lui donnait à manger les plantes à fleurs jaunes qui poussaient à côté de son enclos. Se voyant offrir l'une de ces plantes, Yum Yum la porta à côté de son œil pour vérifier qu'il s'agissait bien de la pâture qu'elle attendait. Le motard, railleur, la traita de « garce aveugle ». Elle s'en alla dignement jusqu'à sa bauge, sans rien laisser paraître de ses sentiments, revint quelques minutes plus tard, repéra le fort en gueule et le doucha d'une boue nauséabonde qu'elle avait emmagasinée dans sa trompe. Cela aurait pu être pire. Yum Yum est cette dame qui n'hésita pas à partager avec nous sa tentative sans aucun doute couronnée de succès de s'inscrire dans le *livre Guinness des records* pour l'ampleur et la durée de ses flatuosités.

Il est plus difficile de savoir quoi penser de Congo, l'éléphant d'Afrique pensionnaire de Western Plains. Celui-ci débuta sa carrière sous les traits de l'éléphanteau dans le film *Hatari.* Vous commencez à travailler avec John Wayne et Howard Hawks, Henry Mancini compose pour vous le thème de « Baby Elephant Walk », et vous vous retrouvez trente-trois ans plus tard au zoo de Dubbo. Ce n'est peut-être pas le destin que Dieu avait prévu pour lui, mais étant donné celui qu'ont connu depuis la plupart des éléphants d'Afrique orientale...

J'éprouve une incertitude analogue quant au fait que nulle photographie de lion (à la différence de la lionne) ne figure dans cette collection. Ce n'est pas faute d'avoir essayé ! Ayant tout simplement décidé de ne pas coopérer, il ne s'est jamais laissé duper pour me donner quelque chose dont j'aurais pu faire un cliché vaguement acceptable. J'en fus réduit, à la longue, à respecter cette détermination.

for you and thirty three years later you're in a Dubbo zoo. It may not be the way God planned it, but given what's happened to most of East Africa's elephants since then...

I have a similar uncertainty about the fact that there's no photograph of a lion (as opposed to a lioness) in this collection. It's not from lack of trying. He just wasn't going to co-operate or even be conned into giving me anything that I could turn into a vaguely acceptable shot. And in the end I had to honour that determination.

Throughout the two-year process of putting this book together, I found that with some notable exceptions I liked best the animals that scared me most. The attitude that sees me as a potential meal gives the relationship an edge. While the crocodile will eat me given much less than half a chance, the herbivorous hippos will kill me just for the hell of it and because that's the way it is. It doesn't matter that they'll also kill each other's young when the mood takes them, there's a purity about their inability to be anything but hippos.

The photograph of the pygmy hippo having tastefully wrapped itself in my backdrop probably has a charm that doesn't quite tell the whole story. Minutes later he defecated all over it—a function that makes hippos' tails spin like rotor blades. He left me with an interestingly tie-dyed canvas and in no doubt that he'd have been just as happy monstering my body parts.

Some of the bigger apes also scared me, but I liked them less. Maybe the evolutionary proximity was the problem. Even the chimps, perhaps the ultimate victims of our anthropomorphic fantasies, seemed threatening. Their aggro was not initially obvious. But when, as is so often the case, youthful curiosity drew

Das Ganze mag zwar nicht besonders gerecht klingen, aber wenn man sich vorstellt, was in dieser Zeit mit den meisten anderen ostafrikanischen Elefanten geschehen ist...

Ebenso gemischte Gefühle bereitet mir die Tatsache, daß diese Sammlung keine Fotografie eines Löwen enthält. Es liegt nicht daran, daß ich es nicht versucht habe: Er war jedoch zu keiner Kooperation bereit und zeigte sich völlig abgeneigt, mir irgendetwas zu geben, das ich in eine einigermaßen annehmbare Aufnahme hätte verwandeln können. Letztendlich mußte ich seine Entschlossenheit anerkennen.

Im Laufe der zwei Jahre, in denen ich dieses Buch zusammenstellte, fand ich heraus, daß ich – von einigen Ausnahmen abgesehen – die Tiere am meisten mochte, die mir besondere Angst einjagten. Ihre Einstellung, mich als eine potentielle Mahlzeit zu betrachten, verlieh unserer Beziehung eine besondere Note. Während das Krokodil mich bei der ersten sich ihm bietenden Gelegenheit auffressen würde, würden die pflanzenfressenden Nilpferde mich aus einer Anwandlung heraus töten — einfach, weil es nun einmal so ist. Denn sie töten sogar gegenseitig ihre Jungen, wenn die Laune sie überkommt — in ihrer Unfähigkeit, etwas anderes sein zu können als Nilpferde, liegt eine gewisse Reinheit.

Die Aufnahme des Zwergflußpferds, das sich geschmackvoll in meinen Hintergrund wickelt, besitzt einen Charme, der nicht die ganze Wahrheit erzählt. Wenige Minuten danach entleerte es seinen Darm über das Tuch — wobei sich der Schwanz des Flußpferds wie ein Rotorblatt zu drehen pflegt. Es hinterließ uns eine Leinwand mit einem interessanten Batikmuster, und ich bin mir sicher, daß es ebenso viel Spaß daran gehabt hätte, meinen Körperteilen etwas Ungeheuerliches anzutun.

Auch einige der größeren Affen jagten mir Angst ein, aber ich konnte sie weniger gut leiden. Vielleicht war die evolutionäre Nähe das Problem. Sogar die Schimpansen, die beliebtesten Opfer unserer anthropomorphen Phantasien, wirkten bedrohlich. Ihre Aggressivität war nicht sofort erkennbar; aber wenn — was häufiger

Au cours des deux années nécessaires à la réalisation de cet ouvrage, j'ai découvert que, sauf quelques exceptions notables, je préférais ceux des animaux qui m'effrayaient le plus. Que je sois considéré comme un repas potentiel, voilà qui aiguisait notre relation. Alors que le crocodile aurait voulu me dévorer à la première occasion, les hippopotames herbivores m'auraient tué sur un simple coup de tête, et parce que c'est comme ça. Peu importe qu'ils massacraient également les rejetons des autres hippopotames si l'envie leur en prenait, il y a une sorte de pureté dans leur incapacité à être autre chose que des hippopotames.

La photographie montrant l'hippopotame nain gracieusement drapé dans ma toile de fond respire probablement un charme qui ne traduit pas exactement la réalité. Quelques minutes plus tard, il déféqua sur tout le tissu — fonction corporelle qu'accompagne le mouvement de sa queue tournant comme un rotor. Il me laissa une toile teinte aux motifs intéressants et aurait indubitablement été aussi heureux de pouvoir m'asperger de la sorte.

Certains des plus grands singes m'effrayaient également, mais je les appréciais moins, le problème étant sans doute leur proximité sur l'échelle de l'évolution. Même les chimpanzés, probablement les dernières victimes de nos fantaisies anthropomorphes, semblaient menaçants. Leur agressivité n'était cependant pas manifeste de prime abord. Mais, comme ce fut si souvent le cas, lorsque la curiosité attirait trop près de moi un jeune singe, les adultes commençaient à se montrer méchants. D'une façon ou d'une autre, leur réaction semblait affectée, comme s'ils cherchaient un prétexte pour engager les hostilités. Somme toute, ils sont trop humains pour notre tranquillité d'esprit, ceci dit en ne tenant pas compte de certaines de leurs habitudes personnelles. Mais ils font de superbes portraits.

Le serpent à sonnettes se livre à un certain battage pour faire sa propre publicité. Avoir entendu durant de nombreuses années le bruit mortel du crotale, soigneusement enregistré et amplifié par Hollywood, ne prépare pas véritablement à

one of their young too close to me. the adults started to turn nasty. And somehow their reaction seemed contrived, as if they wanted an excuse to start trouble. They are altogether too human for comfort, and that's without considering some of their personal habits. However, they make great portraits.

For delivering on its publicity the rattlesnake took some beating. All those years of hearing Hollywood's carefully recorded and enhanced death-rattle doesn't quite prepare you for the rearing fang-to-face reality. The live rattle is somehow worse than the fangs—or the venom, which compensates for its relatively reduced toxicity with sheer volume. On the other hand. the cobra never quite rose to the occasion and it is among the regrettable absentees from the book.

As part of my initiation—and I must have been a tempting target for many of the keepers—I was made to hold the tarantula before I photographed it. I'm not a big hero about spiders and as I was handed the stuff of nightmares I was informed that if you drop a tarantula it'll crack like an egg. That's how it is: you'd rather die of fright than omelette a big. hairy monster.

Confronting dangerous animals who remained unconvinced that I was one of the good guys forced me to face something dark and disturbing within myself. The zoo staff obviously ensured that I was never in any real danger. But through the lens or through the wire the knowledge of safety is easily swept away by fear and adrenalin rush. And that's the dark bit. It's not just that you're afraid—it's the other part of the equation: the 'kill' element of 'kill, or be killed'.

---

vorkam – eines ihrer Jungen voll jugendlicher Neugier zu nah an mich herankam, wurden die Erwachsenen unangenehm. Und irgendwie erschien mir ihre Reaktion gekünstelt, so als ob sie einen Vorwand suchten, um Ärger machen zu können. Sie wirkten viel zu menschlich, um noch Trost gebrauchen zu können – selbst wenn man einige ihrer persönlichen Eigenarten außer acht ließ. Aber sie ergaben großartige Portraits.

Die Klapperschlange ließ einiges über sich ergehen, bevor sie ihr berühmtes Rasseln demonstrierte. Aber selbst wenn man das von Hollywood sorgfältig aufgenommene und verstärkte Todesgeklapper im Ohr hat, ist man nicht auf die hochaufragende Fang-in-Auge-Realität vorbereitet. Dabei ist die echte Klapper irgendwie schlimmer als die Fänge – oder als das Gift, dessen relativ schwache Wirkung durch die Menge kompensiert wird. Die Kobra dagegen zeigte sich der Aufgabe nie wirklich gewachsen und zählt zu den bedauernswerten Abwesenden dieser Sammlung.

Zu meiner Initiation – und ich habe bestimmt für viele Tierpfleger ein verlockendes Ziel geboten – gehörte es, die Tarantel in die Hand zu nehmen, bevor ich sie fotografieren durfte. Wenn es um Spinnen geht, bin ich nicht besonders mutig; aber bevor man mir den fleischgewordenen Alptraum in die Hände drückte, erfuhr ich, daß eine Tarantel wie ein rohes Ei zerbricht, wenn man sie fallen läßt. Also blieb mir nichts anderes übrig: Man stirbt lieber vor Angst, als ein großes, haariges Monstrum zu Omelett zu verarbeiten.

Durch die Begegnung mit gefährlichen Tieren, die sich nicht davon überzeugen ließen, daß ich zu den Guten gehörte, lernte ich eine dunkle und beunruhigende Seite meines Ichs kennen. Natürlich sorgte das Zoopersonal dafür, daß ich mich nie wirklich in Gefahr befand; aber beim Blick durch die Linse oder den Draht kann dieses Bewußtsein der Sicherheit schnell von Angst oder einem Adrenalinstoß hinweggespült werden. Und hier beginnt der dunkle Teil: Man fühlt nicht nur Angst, sondern vor allem den anderen Teil des Gleichnisses – das »Töten« aus »Töten oder getötet werden«.

---

affronter la réalité du serpent dressé, tous crochets dehors, face à votre visage. Le son de crécelle est en quelque sorte plus terrifiant que les crochets, ou que le venin, dont la toxicité relativement faible est compensée par la quantité. D'autre part, jamais le cobra ne se montra véritablement à la hauteur de la situation : il compte au nombre des absences fâcheuses dans cet ouvrage.

En guise d'initiation — et j'ai dû à ce titre représenter une cible bien tentante aux yeux de maints gardiens — il me fallut porter la tarentule avant de la photographier. Je ne suis pas un héros en ce qui concerne les araignées et, alors que je tenais en main l'étoffe des cauchemars, l'on m'informa que si je la laissais tomber par terre, elle se briserait comme un œuf. C'est ainsi : on préférerait mourir de peur plutôt que de faire une omelette d'un énorme monstre poilu.

Affronter des animaux dangereux qui demeuraient parfaitement sceptiques quant au fait que j'étais du côté des bons m'obligea à faire face à quelque chose de sombre et de très troublant tapi en mon for intérieur. Le personnel du zoo avait à l'évidence veillé à ce que jamais je ne sois en situation de réel danger. Pourtant, à travers l'objectif ou la clôture, la certitude que l'on est en sécurité est aisément balayée par la peur et les décharges d'adrénaline. Voilà ce qui est énigmatique. Il ne s'agit pas seulement de peur, mais aussi de l'autre membre de l'équation, le « tuer » dans « tuer, ou être tué ».

Ayant compris cela à tête reposée, j'en vins à avoir quelques lueurs sur la psychologie du chasseur. Je n'en exècre pas moins les salopards qui tuent les animaux pour le plaisir, mais maintenant je sais de quoi est faite leur passion morbide : d'amour-propre, d'orgueil et d'un manque absolu de conscience.

En repensant à tout ce que j'ai vécu pour réaliser les photographies qui composent cette collection, j'éprouve une certaine tristesse, différente du sentiment normalement ressenti après l'amour et qui marque la fin de tout projet intense. Ayant commencé avec la modeste intention de préparer une exposition (ce livre vint ultérieurement), je découvrais que j'avais entrepris quelque chose qui exigeait davantage. Ce n'était pas seulement les compromis techniques et artistiques

With that understanding, albeit recollected in tranquillity. comes a glimmer of insight into the hunter. It doesn't make me hate the bastards who kill wild animals for sport any the less. but now at least I know what their addictive illness tastes like: ego, superiority and a plain lack of awareness.

As I now begin to look back on the whole experience that created this collection I'm touched by a certain sadness. It's different from the normal post-coital feeling that marks the end of all intense projects. Having set out with a modest intention for an exhibition (the book came later) I found that I'd taken on something that demanded more. It wasn't only the technical and creative compromises I had to buy, nor the sense of inadequacy that comes from working around people whose work seems so much more worthwhile than one's own. It was the animals themselves.

As they look out from the photographs—or refuse to—I'm haunted by what they represent about our own arrogance as a species. Originally we kept live animals in captivity for our amusement, sport and curiosity. We grew to marvel at the fact that we could teach many of them tricks—tricks that in themselves were so banal and meaningless as to be worth bugger all. The tricks confirmed our superiority. As someone once said, the Puritans were against bear-baiting not because it was cruel to bears but because it gave pleasure to the people who watched. And there, grace of God and all, seems an accurate indictment of who we have often been in our dealings with the creatures of this shared planet.

Today, as I've said, zoos are the only hope that many of these animals have. The scientific justification that gave us the zoological gardens now has some basis. Having slaughtered them and destroyed their worlds we now offer the survivors sanctuary of a sort. I'm aware that dominant races have behaved

---

In der ruhigen Rückschau vermittelt diese Einsicht einen kleinen Einblick in die Gedanken des Jägers. Natürlich hasse ich die Bastarde, die ein Tier zum Spaß töten, noch genauso wie vorher, aber heute weiß ich zumindest, welche Gefühle aus ihrer Krankheit eine Sucht machen: Ichbezogenheit, Überlegenheitsgefühl und ein schlichter Mangel an Bewußtsein.

Wenn ich heute auf die Erfahrungen dieses Projekts zurückblicke, überfällt mich eine gewisse Traurigkeit; sie unterscheidet sich von den üblichen postkoitalen Gefühlen, die das Ende aller intensiven Fotosessions kennzeichnet. Ich bekam den bescheidenen Wunsch nach einer Ausstellung (das Buch kam später) und entdeckte, daß ich mich auf eine Auseinandersetzung eingelassen hatte, die mir sehr viel abverlangte. Es handelte sich dabei nicht nur um die technischen und kreativen Kompromisse, die ich eingehen mußte, oder um das Gefühl der Unzulänglichkeit, das einen in Gegenwart von Menschen überkommt, deren Arbeit so viel nützlicher ist als die eigene — es waren die Tiere selbst.

Wenn sie mich aus den Fotografien anblicken — oder gerade das verweigern —, verfolgt mich der Gedanke, daß sie uns einen Blick auf die Arroganz unserer eigenen Spezies werfen lassen. Ursprünglich hielten wir lebende Tiere aus Vergnügen, Sport und Neugier in Gefangenschaft. Wir waren begeistert, daß wir vielen von ihnen Kunststückchen beibringen konnten — Kunststückchen, die so banal und sinnlos waren, daß die Tiere wie völlige Idioten dastanden. Und diese Kunststückchen bestätigten unsere Überlegenheit. Jemand hat einmal gesagt, daß die Puritaner nicht deshalb gegen die Bärenhatz waren, weil es den Bären gegenüber grausam sei, sondern weil es den Zuschauern Vergnügen bereiten würde. Und darin liegt — Gottes Gnade hin oder her — das größte Verbrechen, für das wir uns im Umgang mit den anderen Wesen auf diesem gemeinsamen Planeten verantworten müssen.

Heute sind Zoos die einzige Hoffnung, die viele dieser Tiere noch haben. Die wissenschaftliche Begründung für zoologische Gärten bekommt nun tatsächlich eine Grundlage. Nachdem wir sie abgeschlachtet und ihre Welten zerstört haben, bieten wir den Überlebenden eine Art heilige Zufluchtsstätte. Ich bin mir

---

qu'il me fallut faire, ni même ce sentiment d'insuffisance que l'on ressent lorsqu'on travaille avec des gens dont l'activité semble bien plus digne d'éloges que la sienne. C'était les animaux eux-mêmes.

Quand ils nous regardent de leurs photographies — ou refusent de le faire — je suis obsédé par ce qu'ils représentent concernant notre propre arrogance en tant qu'espèce. A l'origine, nous conservions des animaux vivants en captivité pour notre amusement, pour assouvir notre curiosité ainsi que notre goût du sport. Nous avons grandi en nous émerveillant du fait que nous pouvions apprendre à un grand nombre d'entre eux divers tours d'adresse — des trucs si banaux et si dénués de sens que leur seul intérêt, c'était de confirmer notre supériorité. Jadis, les puritains s'opposaient aux combats d'ours et de chiens non parce que c'était cruel envers les ours, mais parce que les spectateurs y prenaient du plaisir. Voilà ce qui, par la grâce de Dieu et de tous ses saints, semble constituer une mise en accusation précise de ce que nous avons souvent été dans nos relations avec les créatures de cette planète partagée.

Aujourd'hui, comme je l'ai déjà dit, les zoos sont le dernier espoir de nombre de ces animaux. Les justifications scientifiques qui ont présidé à la création des jardins zoologiques sont désormais peu ou prou fondées. Après les avoir massacrés et détruit leur univers, nous offrons maintenant aux survivants une sorte de réserve. Je ne suis pas sans ignorer que les races dominantes se sont toujours très mal conduites à l'égard des plus faibles, mais que parfois, du moins en ce qui concerne les êtres humains, les opprimés se vengent. Dans le cas des animaux, il est cependant difficile d'envisager un avenir du type de *La Planète des singes*.

Il n'était pas dans mon intention, à l'origine, de découvrir et d'affronter ma culpabilité humaine au cours de la réalisation de ces images. Mais en chassant de mon esprit les exigences commerciales quotidiennes de la photographie professionnelle, ces animaux et leurs divers caractères m'ont contraint à faire face à quelques vérités relatives à notre place dans l'ordre des choses.

and still behave very badly to weaker people, but at least sometimes with people the cycle turns and the downtrodden get their revenge. It's hard to see any *Planet of the Apes* kind of future for the animals.

It wasn't my intention in the beginning to find and confront my human guilt in the gathering of these images. However, in clearing my head from the day-to-day commercial demands of professional photography, these animals in all their moods forced me to face some truths about our place in the scheme of things.

I may not have learnt patience; the long-suffering zoo staff who made it all possible must, at times, have thought me the strangest creature of all—an impatient though persistent monster. My debt and gratitude to them is enormous, but to the animals it's even greater.

Obviously, I hope that there is pleasure in the photographs and that at least some of them touch you with the emotion that now haunts me: that there's just a little more to them than meets the eye.

**Gary Heery**

Sydney, September 1995

This book is dedicated with admiration, affection and gratitude to the staff of Taronga and Western Plains Zoos.

---

bewußt, daß dominante Rassen sich Schwächeren gegenüber immer so verhalten haben und noch verhalten, aber zumindest bei Menschen läßt sich der Kreislauf umdrehen, und die Unterdrückten bekommen ihre Rache. Allerdings kann ich mir für die Tierwelt keine Zukunft im Stil von *Planet der Affen* vorstellen.

Ursprünglich war es nicht meine Absicht, im Laufe dieses Projekts nach meiner menschlichen Schuld zu suchen und mich damit auseinanderzusetzen. Aber je mehr ich meine Gedanken von den täglichen kommerziellen Anforderungen der professionellen Fotografie befreite, desto mehr zwangen mich die Tiere in all ihren Stimmungen dazu, einigen Wahrheiten über unseren Platz in der Ordnung der Dinge ins Auge zu sehen.

Ich habe immer noch nicht gelernt, mich in Geduld zu üben. Die Mitarbeiter der Zoos, die dieses Projekt überhaupt erst möglich machten, müssen mich zeitweilig für das seltsamste aller Wesen gehalten haben — ein ungeduldiges und dennoch hartnäckiges Monstrum. Ich bin ihnen zu großem Dank verpflichtet — und den Tieren noch mehr.

Und zum Schluß hoffe ich, daß Sie Vergnügen an den Fotografien finden und einige Aufnahmen bei Ihnen das gleiche Gefühl auslösen, das mich nicht mehr losläßt: Hinter diesen Bildern steckt mehr, als man auf den ersten Blick erkennen kann.

**Gary Heery**

Sydney, September 1995

Dieses Buch widme ich voll Bewunderung, Zuneigung und Dankbarkeit den Mitarbeitern der Zoos von Taronga und Western Plains.

---

Je n'y ai sans doute pas appris la patience ; le personnel du zoo, auquel je dois tout et dont la patience fut à toute épreuve, a dû parfois me considérer comme la créature la plus étrange de toutes : un monstre impatient quoique tenace. Si ma dette et ma gratitude sont à leur égard immenses, elles le sont davantage encore à l'égard des animaux.

J'espère bien sûr que l'on prendra plaisir à découvrir ces photographies et que du moins quelques-unes d'entre elles susciteront chez le lecteur l'émotion qui me hante désormais : qu'elles offrent un peu plus que ce que rencontre le regard.

**Gary Heery**

Sydney, septembre 1995

Cet ouvrage est dédié, avec admiration, affection et gratitude, au personnel des zoos de Taronga et de Western Plains.

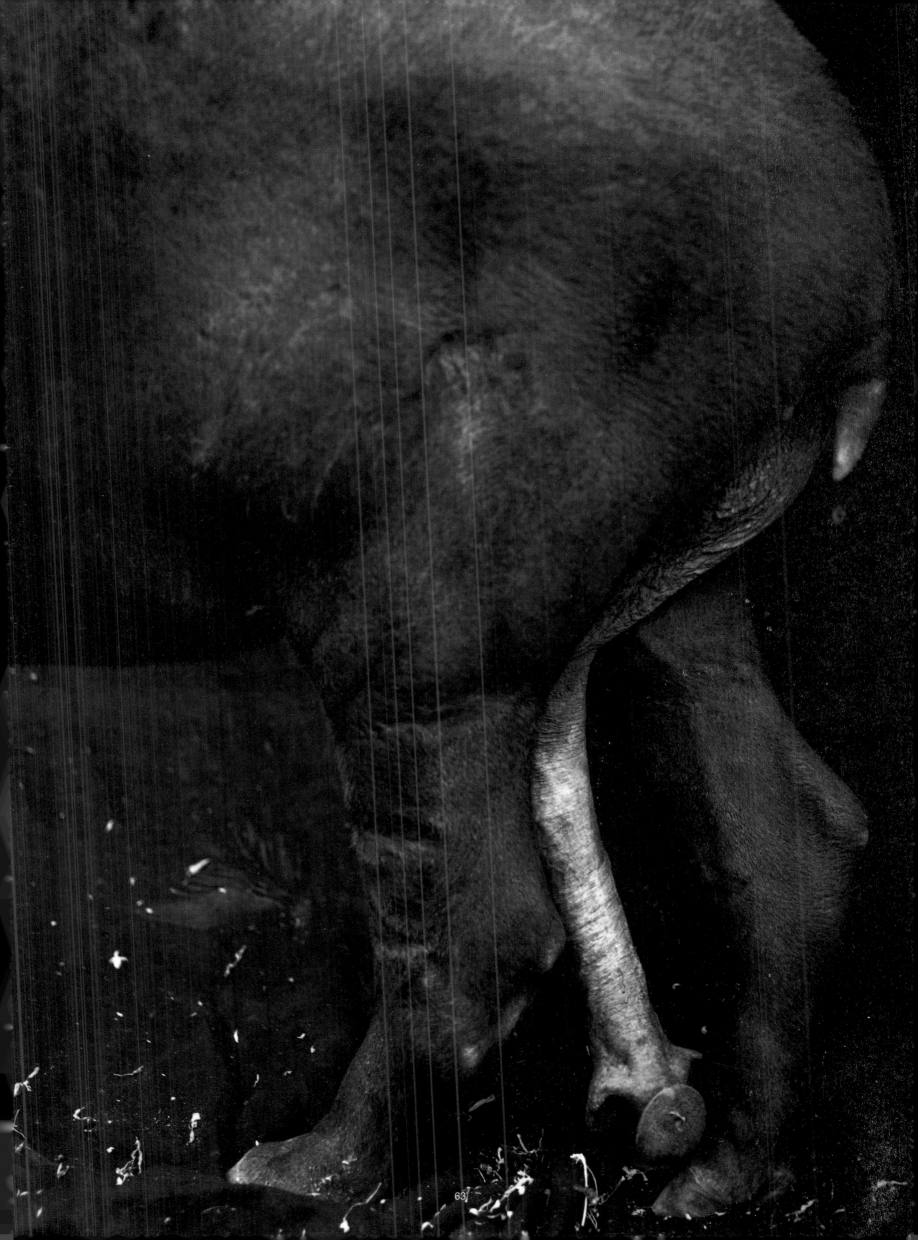

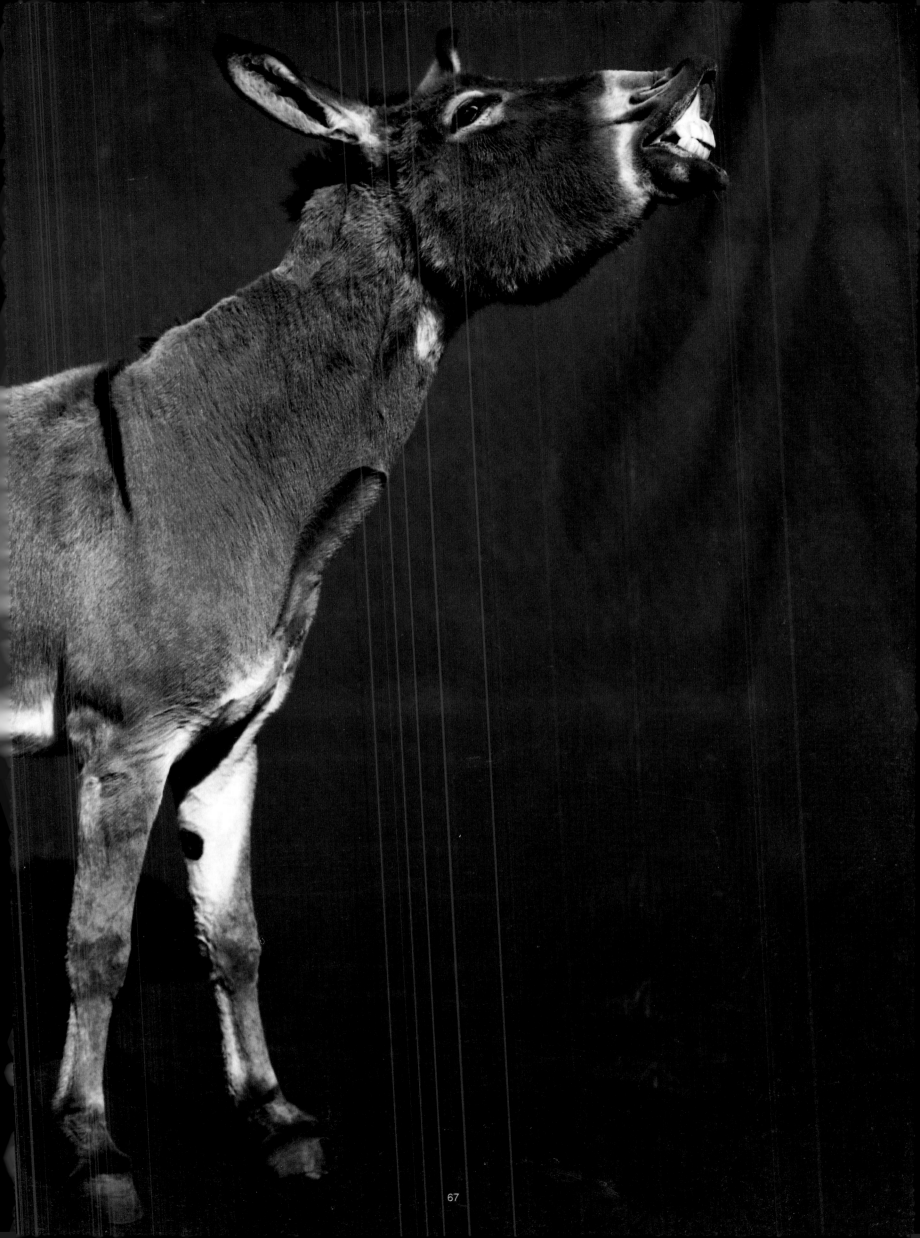

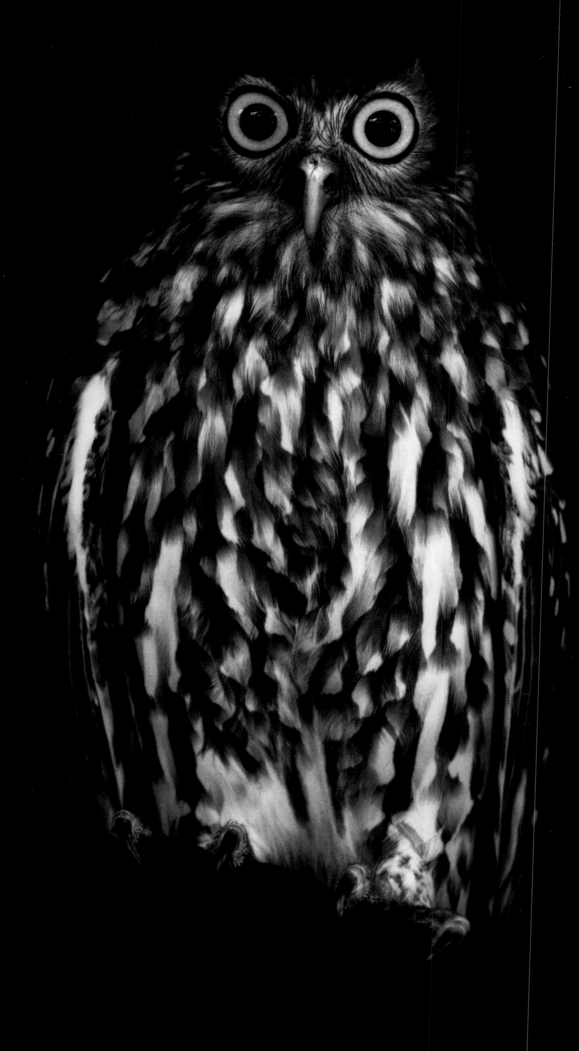

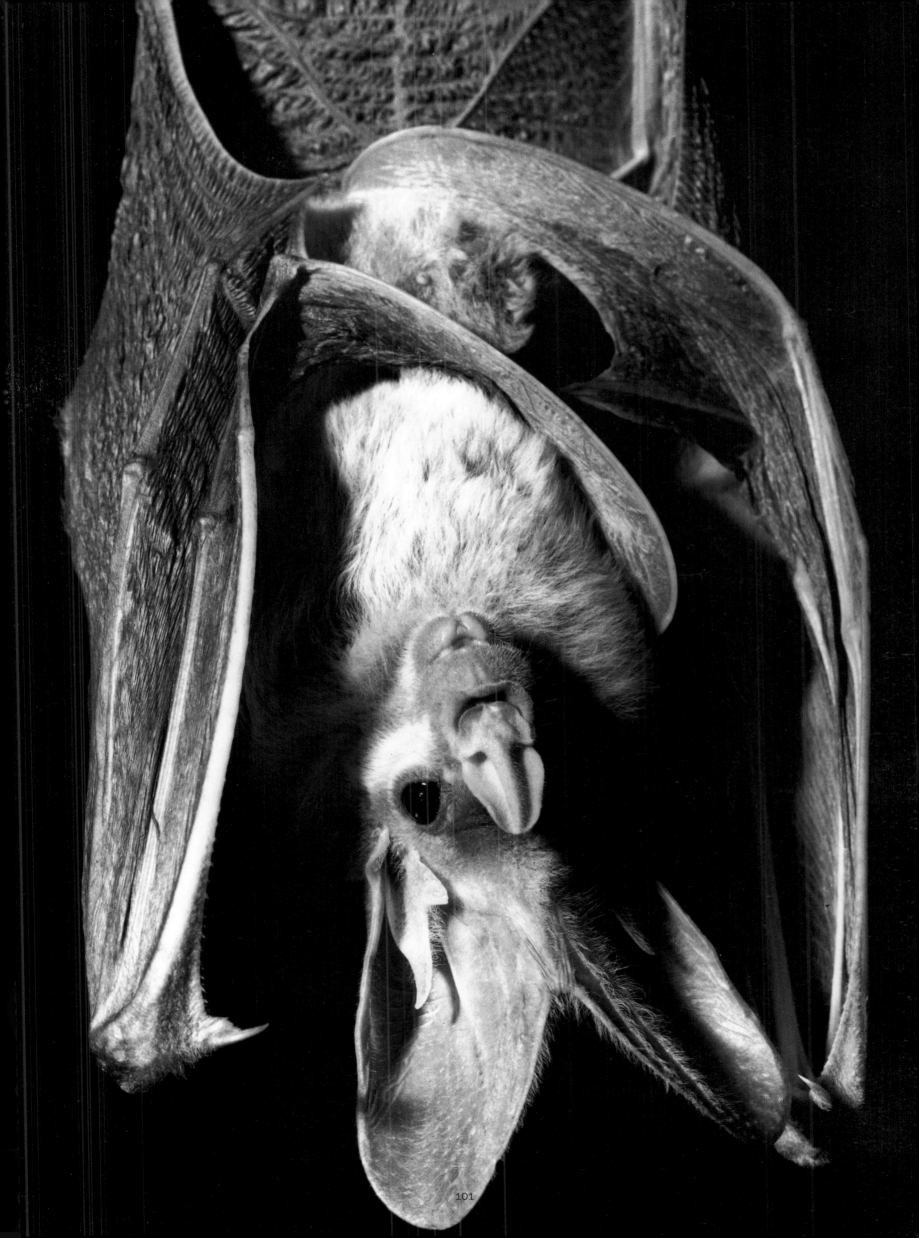

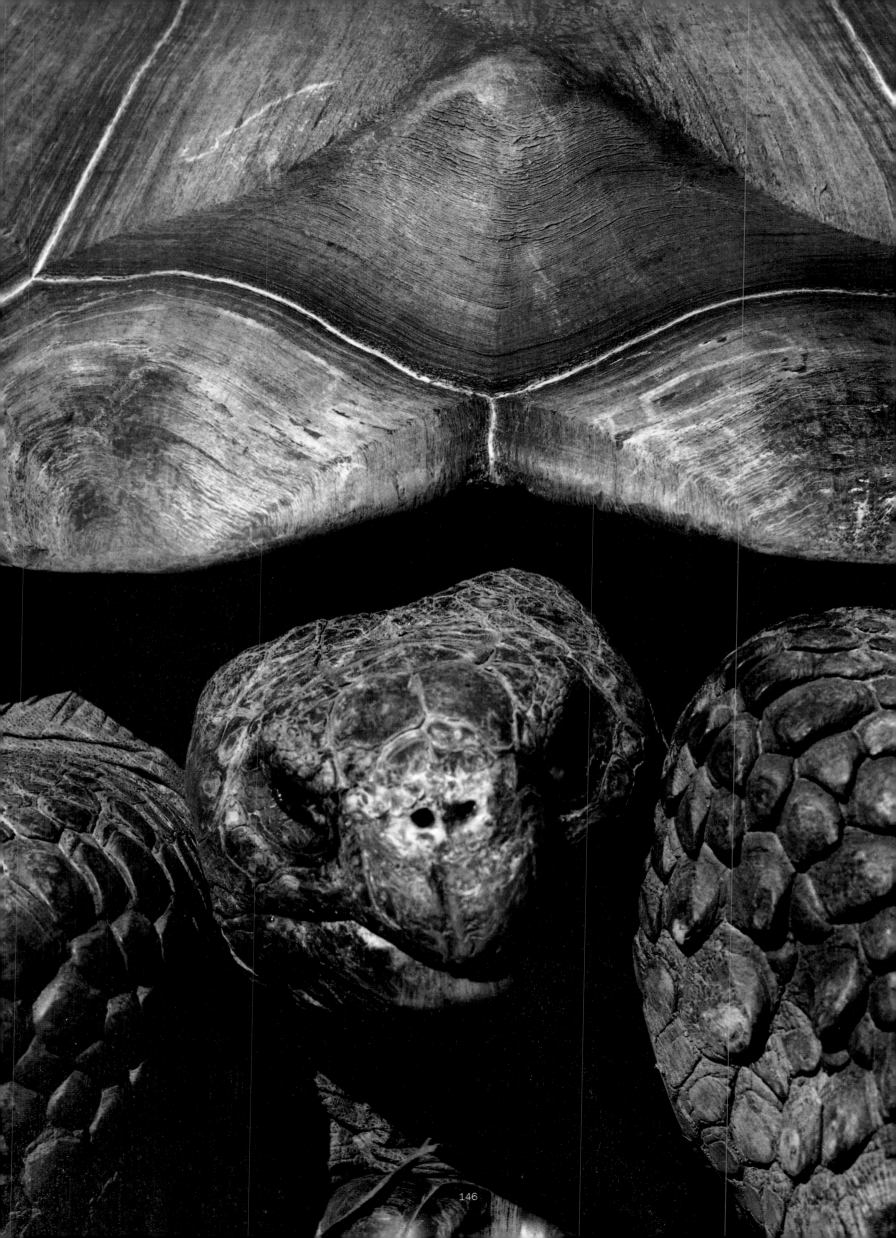

15
Brazilian Tapir, Südamerikanischer
Flachlandtapir, Tapir du Brésil, *Tapirus terrestris*

16
Fallow Deer, Damhirsch, Daim
*Cervus dama*

17
White Tiger, Weißer Tiger, Tigre
*Panthera tigris*

18
Grass Owl, Erdeule, Effraie des prairies
*Tyto longimembris*

19
Diamondback Rattlesnake, Diamantklapper-
schlange, Crotale d'Orient, *Crotalus adamanteus*

20 & 21
Chimpanzee, Schimpanse, Chimpanzé
*Pan troglodytes*

22 & 23
Black Rhinoceros, Spitzmaulnashorn, Rhinocéros
noir, *Diceros bicornis minor*

24 & 25
Emu, Emeu
*Dromaius novahollandiae*

26
Double Plumed basilisk, Stirnlappenbasilisk,
Basilic à aigrette, *Basiliscus plumifrons*

27
Laughing Kookaburra, Lachender Hans, Martin-
chasseur kookaburra, *Dacelo novaeguineae*

28 & 29
Southern Elephant Seal, Südliche Elefantenrobbe,
Eléphant de mer, *Mirounga leonina*

30 & 31
Pygmy Marmoset, Zwergseidenäffchen, Ouistiti
mignon, *Cebuella pygmaea*

32
Southern Rainforest Dragon
*Hypsilurus spinipes*

33
Alpaca, Alpaka
*Lama pacos*

34 & 35
Estuarine Crocodile, Leistenkrokodil, Crocodile
des estuaires, *Crocodylus porosus*

36 & 37
Cheetah, Gepard, Guépard
*Acinonyx jubatus jubatus*

38
Chilean Flamingo, Chile-Flamingo, Flamant du
Chili, *Phoenicopterus chilensis*

39
Mandrill
*Papio sphinx*

40
Emu, Emeu
*Dromaius novaehollandiae*

41
Chilean Rose Tarantula, Tarantel, Tarentule du
Chili, *Grammostola spatulatus*

42 & 43
Slender-tailed Meerkat, Erdmännchen, Merkaat
*Suricata suricatta hahni*

44 & 45
Orang-utan, Orang-Utan, Orang-outang
*Pongo pygmaeus abelii x P. pygmaeus*

46
Blue Peafowl, Pfau, Paon bleu
*Pavo cristatus*

47
Tawny Frogmouth, Eulenschwalm, Podarge fauve
*Podargus strigoides*

48
Black-necked Stork, Riesenstorch, Cigogne à cou noir, *Ephippiorhynchus asiaticus australis*

49
Short-beaked Echidna, Australischer Ameisenigel, Echidné à bec court, *Tachyglossus aculeatus*

50-54
Giraffe, Girafe
*Giraffa camelopardalis*

55
Grass Owl, Erdeule, Effraie du cap
*Tyto capensis*

56-59
Rhinoceros, Nashorn, Rhinocéros
*Ceratotherium simum simum*

60 & 61
Freshwater Crocodile, Australien-Krokodil, Crocodile de Johnstone, *Crocodylus johnstoni*

62
Green Tree Frog, Korallenfinger-Laubfrosch, Grenouille verte, *Litoria caerulea*

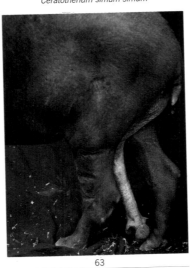

63
Brazilian Tapir, Südamerikanischer Flachlandtapir, Tapir du Brésil, *Tapirus terrestris*

64
Ostrich, Strauß, Autruche
*Struthio camelus*

65
Jackson's Chameleon, Jackson-Chamäleon, Caméléon de Jackson, *Chamaeleo jacksonii*

66 & 67
Donkey, Esel, Ane
*Equus africanus f. asinus*

68 & 69
Chimpanzee, Schimpanse, Chimpanzé
*Pan troglodytes*

70 & 71
Komodo Dragon, Komodo-Waran, Varan de
Komodo, *Varanus komodoensis*

72-74
Sumatran Tiger, Sumatra-Tiger, Tigre de Sumatra
*Panthera tigris sumatrae*

75
Kodiak Bear, Kodiak-Bär, Kodiak
*Ursus arctos middendorffi*

76
Green Python, Grüner Baumpython, Python vert
*Chondropython viridis*

77
Poison Arrow Frog, Färberfrosch, Grenouille
vénimeuse, *Dendrobates tinctorius*

78 & 79
Red Kangaroo, Rotes Riesenkänguruh,
Kangourou roux, *Macropus rufus*

80 & 81
Australian Fur Seal, Südaustralischer Seebär,
Loutre d'Australie, *Arctocephalus pusillus
doriferus*

82
Ring-tailed Lemur, Katta, Maki
*Lemur catta*

83-85
Chapman's Zebra, Chapman-Steppenzebra,
Zèbre de Chapman, *Equus burchelli chapmani*

86
Boa Constrictor, Königsschlange, Boa
constricteur, *Boa constrictor*

87
Turkey, Truthahn, Dindon
*Melleagris gallopavo*

88
Black Swan, Schwarzschwan, Cygne noir
*Chenopis atrata*

89
Mute Swan, Höckerschwan, Cygne muet
*Cygnus olor*

90
Maned Wolf, Mähnenwolf, Loup à crinière
*Chrysocyon brachyurus*

91
Dingo
*Canis familiaris dingo*

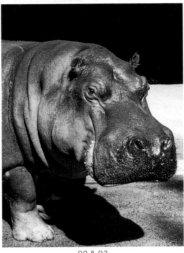

92 & 93
Hippopotamus, Nilpferd, Hippopotame
*Hippopotamus amphibius*

94 & 95
Barking Owl, Kläfferkauz, Chouette glapissante
*Ninox connivens*

96 & 97
Spider Monkey, Geoffroys Klammeraffe, Atèle
*Ateles geoffroyi geoffroyi*

98
Oriental Small-clawed Otter, Klauenloser Otter,
Loutre orientale, *Aonyx cinerea*

99
Grey-headed Flying Fox, Graukopf-Flughund,
Roussette à tête grise, *Pteropus poliocephalus*

100
Double Plumed Basilisk, Stirnlappenbasilisk,
Basilic à aigrette, *Basiliscus plumifrons*

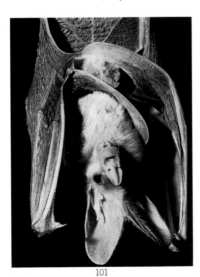

101
Ghost Bat, Gespenst-Fledermaus, Chauve-souris
fantôme, *Macroderma gigas*

102
Hunting Dog, Hyänenhund, Lycaon
*Lycaon pictus*

103
Sugar Glider, Zwerg-Flugbeutler, Pétauriste
*Petaurus breviceps*

104 & 105
Pygmy Hippopotamus, Zwerg-Flußpferd,
Hippopotame nain, *Choeropsis liberiensis*

106 & 107
Arabian Camel, Dromedar, Dromadaire
*Camelus dromedarius*

108
Frilled Lizard, Kragenechse, Lézard à collerette
*Chlamydosaurus kingii*

109
Major Mitchell's Cockatoo, Inka-Kakadu,
Cacatoès Major Mitchell, *Cacatua leadbeateri*

110 & 111
Hippopotamus, Nilpferd, Hippopotame
*Hippopotamus amphibius*

112
Jaguar
*Panthera onca*

113
Green Tree Frog, Korallenfinger-Laubfrosch,
Grenouille verte, *Litoria caerulea*

114
Koala
*Phascolarctos cinereus cinereus*

115
Sulphur-crested Cockatoo, Gelbhauben-Kakadu,
Cacatoès à huppe jaune, *Cacatua galerita*

116-119
African Elephant, Afrikanischer Elefant, Eléphant
d'Afrique, *Loxodonta africana*

120
Scimitar Oryx, Säbelantilope, Oryx scimitar
*Oryx dammah*

121
Water Buffalo, Wasserbüffel, Arni
*Bubalus arnee*

122
Koala
*Phascolarctos cinereus cinereus*

123
Common Wombat, Nacktnasenwombat, Wombat
*Vombatus ursinus*

124
Rufous Owl, Rostkauz, Chouette rousse
*Ninox rufa*

125
Black Cockatoo, Raben-Kakadu, Cacatoès noir
*Calyptorhynchus banksii*

126
American Bison, Bison, Bison d'Amérique
*Bison bison*

127
Tiger, Tigre
*Panthera tigris*

128
Lace Monitor, Buntwaran, Varan à collier
*Varanus varius*

129
Eastern Barred Bandicoot, Tasmanischer Lang-
nasenbeutler, Pèramèle oriental, *Perameles gunnii*

130
Emperor Tamarin, Kaiserschnurrbart-Tamarin,
Tamarin empereur, *Saguinus imperator
subgrisescens*

131
Golden Lion Tamarin, Goldgelbes Löwenäffchen,
Tamarin à crinière de lion, *Leontopithecus rosalia
rosalia*

132
Common or Eastern Bearded Dragon, Bart-
Agame, Varan oriental, *Pogona varbatus*

133
Brolga, Brolga-Kranich, Grue rubiconde
*Grus rubicunda*

134
Goat, Ziege, Chèvre
*Capra aegargus*

135
Chicken, Huhn, Poule
*Gallus gallus*

136
Spotted Deer, Tüpfelhirsch, Axis
*Cervus axis axis*

137
Green and Gold Bell Frog, Goldlaubfrosch,
Grenouille dorée, *Litoria aurea*

138
Guanaco, Guanako
*Lama guanicoe*

139
Common Brush-tail Possum, Langohriger
Fuchskusu, Opossum, *Trichosurus vulpecula*

140
New Zealand Fur Seal, Neuseeland-Seebär,
Loutre de Nouvelle-Zélande, *Arctocephalus
forsteri*

141
Tasmanian Devil, Beutelteufel, Diable de
Tasmanie, *Sarcophilus harrisii*

142
Bilby, Ohrenbeuteldachs
*Macrotis lagotis*

143
Siamang
*Hylobates syndactylus*

144 & 145
Cotton Top Tamarin, Baumwollkopf-Tamarin,
Tamarin, *Saguinus oedipus oedipus*

146 & 147
Galapagos Tortoise, Galapagos-Riesenschildkröte,
Tortue des Galapagos, *Geochelone elephantopus*

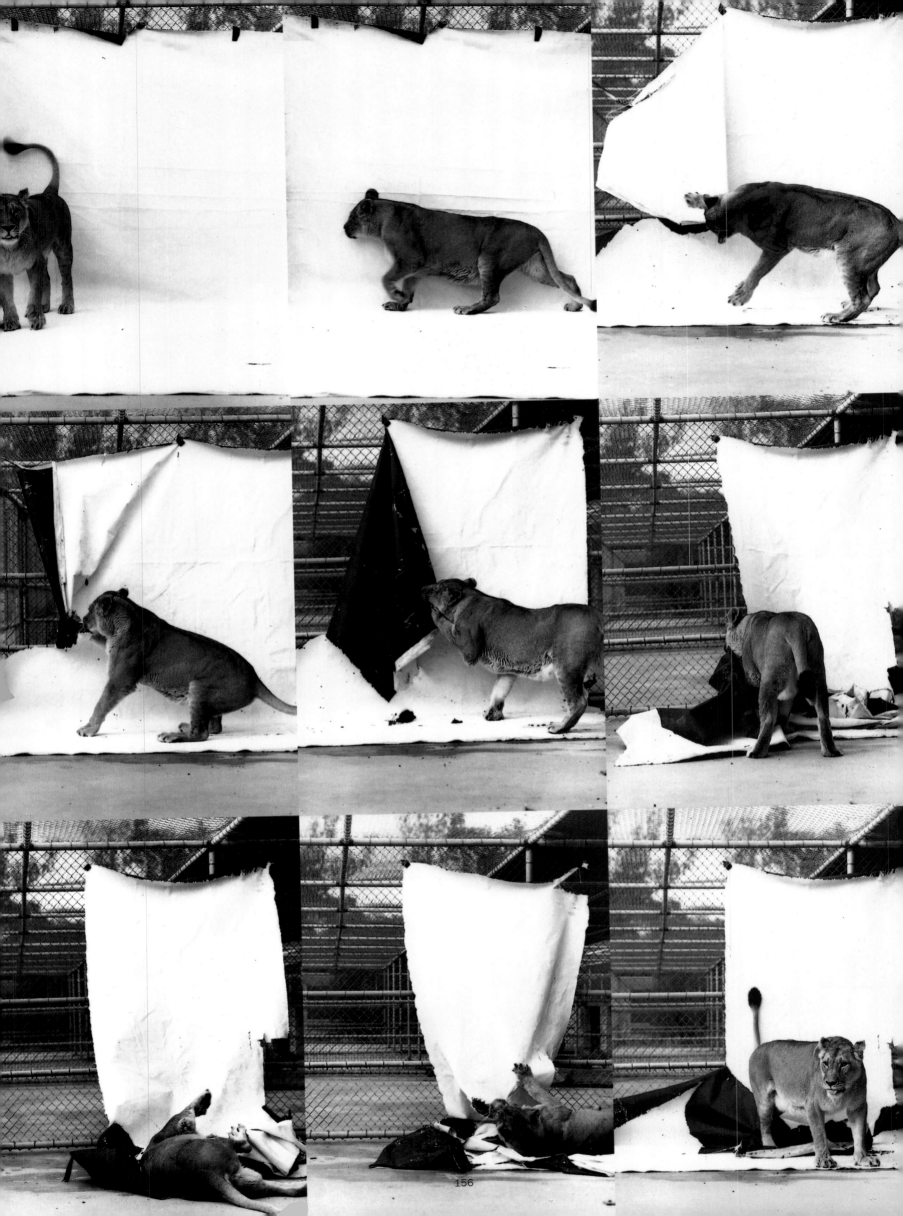

157
Lion
*Panthera leo persica X L leo*

Acknowledgements

I would like to thank the following for their

valuable assistance:

Rosemary Sharman at Kodak Australia Pty Ltd.,

David Lynch at Maxwell Optical Industries, Jayne

Ashbrook at Polaroid Australia Pty Ltd and Jane

Palfreyman at Random House.


Special thanks go to my assistants,

Guy Heritage and Omee Deling,

and also Robert Young and Brett Monahagn.

In the darkroom, Susie Wood

and her assistant Brent S. Young from

The Cusom Darkroom.

At the Zoo, Darril Clements, Katie Tubbs

and Carol Inkson

Technical Information

Camera – RZ67 Mamyia

Lenses – 65mm, 110mm, 180mm, 250mm

Film – Polaroid 100, Plus X 120, TriX 120

Paper – Kodak Polymax Fineart

Paper developer – Kodak Polymax T Developer

Film developer – Kodak D-76 1:1

Danksagung

Ich möchte mich für die wertvolle Unterstützung

bedanken bei:

Rosemary Sharman, Kodak Australia Pty Ltd.;

David Lynch, Maxwell Optical Industries; Jayne

Ashbrook, Polaroid Australia Pty Ltd. und Jane

Palfreyman, Random House.


Besonderer Dank gilt meinen Assistenten

Guy Heritage und Omee Deling

sowie Robert Young und Brett Monahagn.

In der Dunkelkammer: Susie Wood

und ihr Assistent Brent S. Young,

The Cusom Darkroom.

Im Zoo: Darril Clements, Katie Tubbs

und Carol Inkson.

Technische Informationen

Kamera - RZ67 Mamyia

Objektive - 65 mm, 110 mm, 180 mm, 250 mm

Film - Polaroid 100, Plus X 120, TriX 120

Papier - Kodak Polymax Fineart

Papierentwickler - Kodak Polymax T Developer

Filmentwickler - Kodak D-76 1:1

Remerciements

Je souhaite remercier ici les personnes suivantes

pour leur aide précieuse :

Rosemary Sharman de Kodak Australia Pty Ltd.,

David Lynch de Maxwell Optical Industries, Jayne

Ashbrook de Polaroid Australia Pty Ltd. et Jane

Palfreyman de Random House.


Que soient plus particulièrement remerciés mes

assistants, Guy Heritage et Omee Deling,

ainsi que Robert Young et Brett Monahagn.

Dans la chambre noire, Susie Wood

et son assistant Brent S. Young de

The Cusom Darkroom.

Au zoo, Darril Clements, Katie Tubbs

et Carol Inkson.

Précisions techniques

Appareil - Mamyia RZ67

Objectifs - 65 mm, 110 mm, 180 mm, 250 mm

Pellicule - Polaroid 100, Plus X 120, Tri X 120

Papier - Kodak Polymax Fineart

Révélateur papier - Kodak Polymax T Developer

Révélateur film - Kodak D-76 1:1

Originally published by
**Random House Australia Pty Ltd**
20 Alfred Street, Milsons Point, NSW 2061

First published in 1996
Copyright © Gary Heery

Original title: Zoo: a black and white portrait


© 1997 for this edition
Könemann Verlagsgesellschaft mbH
Bonner Str. 126, D–50968 Köln
German translation:   Franca Fritz, Heinrich Koop
French translation:     Christian Diebold
Typesetting:              Oliver Hessmann, Birgit Beyer
Production manager: Detlev Schaper
Printing and binding: Mateu Cromo
Printed in Spain
ISBN 3-89508-535-9

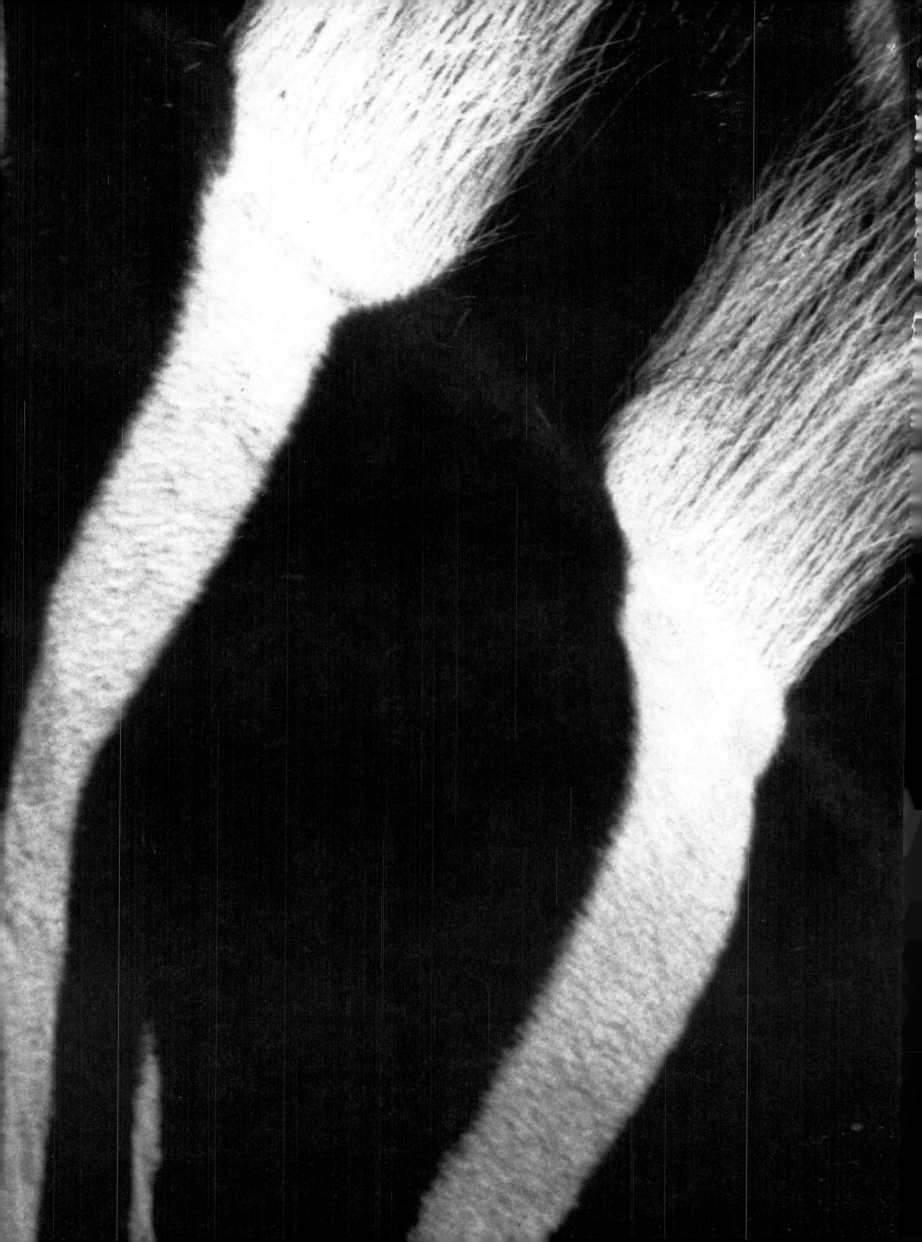